ARMADILLOS

ARMADILLOS

DON PATTON
THE CHILD'S WORLD

As the sun begins to descend behind the western hills, a strange-looking animal begins to emerge from its burrow. Its heavy, bony armor and clawed limbs give it an almost prehistoric look. It begins to root around in the soft soil with its snout. With great determination, it claws at the soil to move a rock and is rewarded with a juicy selection of insects and worms. It eats them quickly and then clumsily wanders toward the next patch of soft soil.

Although reptilian in appearance, this animal is not some miniature relative of the long-extinct dinosaurs. Instead, it's a mammal known as an *armadillo*.

Armadillo is a Spanish word that means "little armored one." The armadillo has also been called "grave digger" and "poor man's pig" because of its strange behavior and odd appearance. Armadillos were called "turtle rabbits" by the Aztec Indians because of their rabbitlike ears and turtlelike shells.

Armadillos are part of a group of mammals called Edentata. Anteaters and sloths are also members of this group. Edentates are among the most primitive mammals in North, Central, and South America. The armadillo is the most primitive of the edentates—it has roamed the earth for the last 55 million years!

There are twenty-one species of armadillos in the world, ranging in size from the tiny pink *fairy armadillo* (only five inches long and weighing a mere three ounces) to the *giant armadillo* (thirty-nine inches long and weighing 110 pounds). The only armadillo found in the United States is the *nine-banded armadillo*, which is fifteen to seventeen inches long and weighs eight to seventeen pounds.

Armadillos are very sensitive to outside temperatures. They cannot survive long periods of frost or even occasional cold weather. Under cold conditions an armadillo's heating system cannot warm the animal fast enough for normal functions. If the cold lasts long enough, the armadillo's body begins to shut down and the animal dies.

Because of their sensitivity to cold, armadillos are found only in semitropical and tropical areas. They are common in the southern United States, Mexico, all of Central America, and South America east of the Andes Mountains.

During the hot summer months, an armadillo spends most of the day sleeping in its cool underground burrow. At night, when the temperature is cooler, it comes out to hunt and eat. In winter it reverses this schedule, foraging during the warm afternoon hours and spending the cold winter nights sleeping within the warm protection of its burrow. By changing its feeding and sleeping times in this way, the armadillo can help its body maintain a constant temperature.

Since tropical areas are sometimes hit by flash floods or heavy rains, most species of armadillos have developed the ability to swim. The champion swimmer is the nine-banded armadillo common in the United States. By taking many deep breaths, the animal fills its stomach and intestines with air. The armadillo can then float at the surface while it dogpaddles its way across the swollen river or stream. Armadillos can hold their breath for up to six minutes, so sometimes they simply walk along the bottom of a waterway!

Armadillos can live in a variety of areas, called *habitats*, as long as they have soft soil, warm weather, water to drink, and a steady supply of worms and insects to eat. Soft soil is the most important feature of an armadillo habitat, for it allows the animal to dig a burrow.

An armadillo's burrow provides shelter from the weather and protection from predators. An armadillo usually has several of these burrows. The deep burrow it uses as its main home provides shelter from very cold or very hot temperatures. The animal then digs a number of shallow burrows around its home so it can dart quickly into a protected place when a predator gets too near.

Armadillos mate at the end of summer. The babies *gestate*, or grow, inside the mother for eight months. During this time she builds a nest inside the home burrow using dry grass and leaves. The mother gives birth in the spring and usually has four babies, called *pups*. The four pups are either all males or all females, and are identical in appearance and size.

The pups are active from the moment of birth. They are born with their eyes open and can walk within a few hours! For the first two weeks they are happy drinking their mother's milk inside the comfort and protection of the home burrow. Within a few weeks they are hunting for insects and worms under their mother's watchful eye. Eventually the soft, pink armor they are born with begins to harden. Within months the pups are almost the same size as their mother.

The armadillo uses its sensitive sense of smell to search for food in the soft soil. It can smell an insect or worm buried eight inches underground! It digs at the ground with its sharp and powerful claws. Once it uncovers the food, the armadillo laps up the insects with its tongue, which has small bumps and is covered with sticky saliva so that the insects will stick to it. Although its diet consists mostly of insects and worms, it also eats spiders, scorpions, snails, and occasionally plant shoots, small snakes, fruit, roots, bird eggs, and dead animals.

The armadillo has two ways of escaping or avoiding predators. When startled, it can avoid a charging animal by leaping high into the air and then scurrying into the safety of one of its many burrows. If caught out in the open, however, the armadillo curls itself into a tight ball, leaving nothing but hard bony armor exposed to the would-be predator. Usually the intruder leaves frustrated—and with an empty stomach.

The major predators that hunt armadillos include foxes, coyotes, wolves, bobcats, cougars, pet dogs, and even humans. In many countries, including the United States, armadillo meat is considered quite good. The taste is said to be similar to pork. The armadillo's tough bony hide is often made into baskets or handbags.

Armadillos, with their bony armored bodies, armored tails, piglike eyes, rabbitlike ears, and clawed legs, are strange and primitive-looking animals. In their 55 million years on the planet, they have developed behaviors that have helped them to survive—yet their appearance has remained mostly unchanged. It is certainly one of nature's most amazing animals!

INDEX

PHOTO RESEARCH
Jim Rothaus/James R. Rothaus & Associates

PHOTO EDITOR
Robert A. Honey / Seattle

PHOTO CREDITS
Joe McDonald: front cover,24
Jeff Foott: 2,4,8,21
Norbert Wu: 7,13,17,22,28
WIDE WORLD PHOTOS: 11
Leonard Lee Rue III: 14,18,27
Robert & Linda Mitchell: 31

Library of Congress Cataloging-in-Publication Data
Patton, Don
Armadillos / Don Patton.
p. cm.
Includes index.
ISBN 1-56766-182-3
(hardcover, reinforced library binding : alk. paper)
1. Armadillos – Juvenile literature
[1. Armadillos.] I. Title.
QL737.E23P38 1995   95-7179
599.3'1 – dc20   CIP
                                      AC